ANIMALS

Zebras

by Kevin J. Holmes

Consultant:
Debora Clem
Education Resource Coordinator
Zoo Atlanta

Bridgestone Books
an imprint of Capstone Press
Mankato, Minnesota

Bridgestone Books are published by Capstone Press
151 Good Counsel Drive, P.O. Box 669, Mankato, Minnesota 56002
http://www.capstone-press.com

Library of Congress Cataloging-in-Publication Data
Holmes, Kevin J.
    Zebras/by Kevin J. Holmes.
    p. cm.—(Animals)
    Includes bibliographical references (p. 23) and index.
    Summary: An introduction to zebras, covering their physical characteristics, habits,
food, and relationship to humans.
    ISBN 0-7368-0497-8
    1. Zebras—Juvenile literature. [1. Zebras] I. Title. II. Animals (Mankato, Minn.)
QL737.U62 H65 2000
599.665'7—dc21   99-053971

Editorial Credits
Erika Mikkelson, editor; Timothy Halldin, cover designer; Kimberly Danger, photo
  researcher

Photo Credits
Craig Brandt, 20
Elizabeth DeLaney, 16
KAC Productions/Peter Gottschling, 6
Michael Turco, 12
Michele Burgess, 4, 8
Photri-Microstock/M.M. Bruce, 18
Robin Brandt, cover
Visuals Unlimited/Corinne Humphrey, 10; Leonard Lee Rue III, 14

1 2 3 4 5 6 05 04 03 02 01 00

Table of Contents

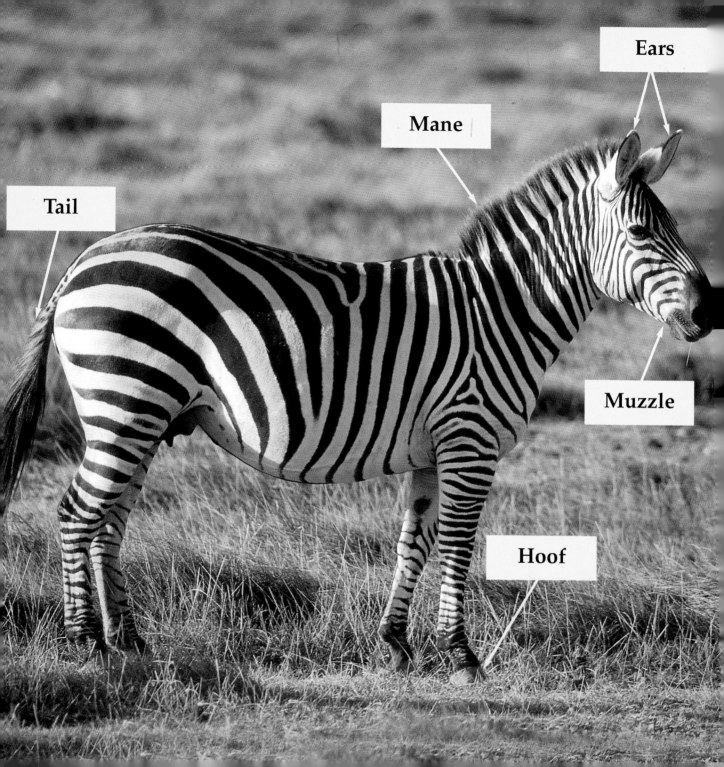

Ears

Mane

Tail

Muzzle

Hoof

Fast Facts

Kinds: The three species of zebras are the plains zebra, the Grevy's zebra, and the mountain zebra.

Range: Zebras live in Africa.

Habitat: Zebras live in semi-deserts, savannas, and rocky areas. Savannas are flat, grassy areas with few trees. Semi-deserts receive more rainfall each year than deserts.

Food: Zebras eat grass, shrubs, herbs, and bark.

Mating: Male zebras must fight with other males in order to win a mate. Most foals are born in the spring.

Young: Young zebras are called foals. Foals have brown and white stripes. Female zebras become adults at age 2. Males reach adulthood when they are 5 or 6 years old.

Zebras

Zebras are easy animals to recognize. Zebras are horselike animals with black and white stripes.

Zebras are mammals. Mammals are warm-blooded animals with backbones. The body heat of warm-blooded animals does not change with the weather. Female mammals feed milk to their young.

Three species of zebras live in the world. They are the plains zebra, the Grevy's zebra, and the mountain zebra. All three species of zebras live in Africa. Thousands of plains zebras live throughout Africa. Fewer mountain zebras and Grevy's zebras live in the wild. Their habitats have been destroyed by people who farm the land.

Horses, donkeys, and wild asses are relatives of the zebra. Zebras are shorter than horses. Zebras also have smaller hooves. The zebra's mane of hair is shorter and stands up more than a horse's mane.

Zebras stand 4 to 5 feet (1 to 1.5 meters) tall at the shoulder.

Appearance

All zebras have stripes. Zebras have black and white stripes. Zebra foals have brown stripes. Zebras sometimes have yellow or gray stripes between the black and white stripes. Each zebra has its own pattern of stripes. No two zebras look exactly alike.

Zebras have similar characteristics. All zebras have long, narrow legs. Their faces are long. They have a black or brown snout with two large nostrils. Zebras also have a long tail. A mane of hair stretches down the back of the zebra's neck.

Plains zebras are the heaviest of all zebras. They have short legs and black muzzles. A muzzle is the nose, mouth, and jaws of an animal.

Grevy's zebras are the tallest zebras. They have narrow stripes. Their ears are longer and rounder than other zebras' ears.

Mountain zebras are the smallest of all zebras. They have brown muzzles and long, pointed ears.

Each zebra has a different stripe pattern.

Homes

Scientists believe zebras once lived in Europe. Today, zebras are found only in Africa. Plains zebras live in central and eastern Africa. They live on grasslands called savannas. Grevy's zebras live in the low hill country or dry semi-deserts of northeast Africa.

Mountain zebras live in national parks or on reserves in southern Africa. These areas protect zebras from hunters. The land is rocky in southern Africa. Mountain zebras are excellent climbers.

Most zebras live in herds. The herd consists of a male zebra, one to six female zebras, and their foals. Male zebras are called stallions. Young stallions often travel in herds without any females.

When the herd travels, the oldest female zebra leads the group. She is called the senior mare. The stallion usually walks behind the other mares and foals.

Zebra herds share the African savannas with antelope.

Food

Zebras are herbivores. Herbivores eat only plants. They eat grasses, shrubs, herbs, and bark.

Zebras' mouths are suited for eating grass and plants. Zebras have soft, flexible lips that gather the food they eat.

The food the zebra eats is hard on its teeth. Zebras' teeth wear down as they chew on bark and shrubs. Zebras grow new teeth to replace the old teeth. A zebra's teeth continue to grow until the zebra dies.

Zebras spend most of the day grazing. They graze on the grasses and plants in an area. At other times, zebras rest, play, or look for more food.

Zebras search for food and water during the dry season. They may walk 100 miles (161 kilometers) in a single day. Plains zebras and Grevy's zebras need water every 36 hours. Mountain zebras can drink water only once every three or four days and survive.

Zebras living on the deserts and savannas spend most of their time looking for water.

Defenses

Zebras must protect themselves from many dangerous predators. Hyenas, jackals, wild dogs, lions, and leopards hunt zebras. Zebras are aware of their surroundings. They often see, smell, and hear danger before it approaches.

Zebras work together to protect each other. Their stripes blend together when they stand in a group. The mixing of stripes makes it difficult for predators to see the zebras. Two zebras standing side-by-side usually face opposite directions. The two zebras then can watch for danger in all directions.

One zebra stands guard while the others eat or rest. The zebra guard warns the herd if any predators are near. The zebras then run away.

Running is the zebra's best defense. Zebras can run very fast for long periods of time. Zebras run as fast as 40 miles per hour (64 kilometers per hour). Most predators cannot keep up with them.

Zebras stand facing opposite directions to watch for possible attackers.

Mating and Young

A zebra mare is ready to mate when she is 2 years old. Zebras mate to produce young. Mares mate only with the stallion in their herd.

Mating can take place at any time during the year. A female zebra gives birth 12 to 13 months after mating. She leaves the group to find a private place to give birth. Mares can give birth every three years.

Young zebras have brown and white stripes. They are called foals. They stand up within the first 15 minutes of life. Foals can walk by the end of their first hour of life.

Newborn foals stay close to their mothers. The mother keeps other zebras away from the foal for the first days. The mother warns the foal when danger is near. The foal then must be ready to run with the rest of the group.

Zebra foals weigh about 70 pounds (32 kilograms) at birth.

Stallions

Young zebras quickly learn the rules of the herd. They must learn their rank among the group. They also must learn how to protect themselves. Young zebras learn these skills by playing with each other and with other adults.

Foals are ready to leave the herd in one to three years. Male zebras leave the group and join other young male zebras.

A young stallion must find a mare to start his own herd. The only mares available are already protected by other stallions. The young stallion must steal a mare from another stallion.

Stallions usually must fight other stallions to steal a mare. The stallions stomp the ground and snort at each other. They then bite, kick, and neck wrestle. Zebras neck wrestle by twisting their necks together. The fight continues until one of the zebras gives up the battle.

Stallions fight to steal a mare away from a herd.

Zebras and People

Millions of zebras once lived throughout Africa. The number of zebras has dropped over the last 50 years. People kill zebras illegally. Hunters shoot zebras and sell their hides for money. People also hunt zebras for meat.

Other zebras die because they have no place to live. Humans farm the land where these zebras once lived. Fewer zebras can survive in Africa without space to run and food to eat.

Some zebras are endangered. Few Grevy's zebras and mountain zebras are left in the wild. For now, the plains zebras are not in danger. They still have land to live on and food to eat.

People are working to protect all three kinds of zebras. People have set up national parks and reserves in Africa. Zebras who live in these protected areas are safe. Africans also have made zebra hunting illegal.

Zebras are protected from hunters in national parks.

Hands On: Fingerprints

Zebra stripes are as different as human fingerprints. All zebras have different patterns of stripes on their bodies. Each human has a unique set of fingerprints. You can compare your fingerprints with your friends' fingerprints.

What You Need

Washable ink pad
White notebook paper
Magnifying glass
Friends

What You Do

1. Press your thumb down on the ink pad.
2. Press your thumb on the piece of paper.
3. Do this a few times in different spots on the paper.
4. Ask your friends to do the same on their own pieces of paper.
5. Use the magnifying glass to look at your fingerprints. Notice the pattern of your fingerprint. Compare it to your friends' fingerprints. How are they different?

Words to Know

endangered (en-DAYN-jurd)—placed in a dangerous situation; animals are endangered when few are left in the wild.

foal (FOHL)—a young zebra

herbivore (HUR-buh-vor)—an animal that eats only plants

mammal (MAM-uhl)—a warm-blooded animal with a backbone that feeds milk to its young

mane (MAYN)—the long, thick hair on the head and neck of a zebra

mate (MAYT)—to join together to produce young

predator (PRED-uh-tur)—an animal that hunts and eats other animals

savanna (suh-VAN-uh)—a flat, grassy area with few or no trees

Read More

Denis-Huot, Christine. *The Zebra, Striped Horse.* Animal Close-ups. Watertown, Mass.: Charlesbridge, 1999.

Fredericks, Anthony D. *Zebras.* Early Bird Nature Books. Minneapolis: Lerner, 2000.

Grimbly, Shona. *Zebras.* Endangered! New York: Benchmark Books, 1999.

Useful Addresses

The Oakland Zoo
P.O. Box 5238
Oakland, CA 94605

The San Antonio Zoo
3903 N. St. Mary's Street
San Antonio, TX 78212-3199

Internet Sites

Wild Lives—Zebras
http://www.awf.org/animals/zebra.html

Zebra Information Project
http://planetpets.simplenet.com/plntzbra.htm

Index